Let's Investigate Plants!

How Plants Make and Spread Seeds

By Ruth Owen

KidHaven PUBLISHING

Published in 2024 by
KidHaven Publishing, an Imprint of Greenhaven Publishing, LLC
2544 Clinton St., Buffalo, NY 14224

Portions of this work were originally authored by Ruth Owen and published as *How Do Plants Make and Spread Their Seeds?*
All new material this edition authored by Ruth Owen.

Produced for Rosen by Ruby Tuesday Books Ltd
Editor for Ruby Tuesday Books Ltd: Mark J. Sachner
US Editor: Designer: Emma Randall

Photo Credits:
Cover, 1, 4, 5 (top), 6–7, 8–9, 10–11, 13, 14 (bottom), 15 (top), 16, 17 (bottom), 18–19, 20–21, 22–23, 24–25, 26–27, 28–29 © Shutterstock; 5 (bottom), 14 (top), 15 (bottom right) © FLPA; 12, 15 (bottom left) © Wikipedia Creative Commons; 17 (top) © Science Photo Library.

Cataloging-in-Publication Data

Names: Owen, Ruth.
Title: How plants make and spread seeds / Ruth Owen.
Description: Buffalo, New York : KidHaven Publishing, 2024. | Series: Let's investigate plants! | Includes glossary and index.
Identifiers: ISBN 9781534545632 (pbk.) | ISBN 9781534545649 (library bound) | ISBN 9781534545656 (ebook)
Subjects: LCSH: Seeds--Juvenile literature. | Seeds--Dispersal--Juvenile literature.
Classification: LCC QK661.O94 2024 | DDC 581.4'67--dc23

Manufactured in the United States of America

CPSIA compliance information: Batch #CSKH24: For further information contact Greenhaven Publishing LLC at 1-844-317-7404.

Please visit our website, www.greenhavenpublishing.com.
For a free color catalog of all our high-quality books, call toll free 1-844-317-7404 or fax 1-844-317-7405.

Find us on

Contents

Making New Plants

Peas, peanuts, kidney beans, acorns—all these things look very different. However, they are all the same in one important way: They are all seeds that can become new plants.

Some seeds, like those produced by orchids, are so tiny they look like specks of dust. Others grow much larger. In fact, the largest seeds on Earth are the size of a basketball. These enormous seeds, which come from the coco de mer palm tree, often weigh up to 40 pounds (18 kg) each!

Large or small, every seed contains all the material needed to grow a new plant. Most seeds form inside flowers. Some grow inside **cones**.

So how do plants grow their seeds, and how does a seed make the journey from its parent plant to its eventual growing place?

marigold

marigold seeds

coco de mer palm tree seed

How to Make a Seed

Many plants grow their seeds inside flowers. This includes many species, or types, of trees.

A flower has male parts called **stamens**. Each stamen is made up of a filament and an **anther**. The female part of a flower is called the **pistil**. Each pistil is made up of a **stigma**, a stalk called a style, and an **ovary**. Making seeds begins with **pollination** of a plant's flowers. The **pollen** made by the anthers of one flower must be carried to the stigma of another flower of the same species. Pollen can be carried from flower to flower by the wind or on the body of an animal, such as a bee.

apple tree flowers

a honeybee covered with yellow pollen

Once a flower has been pollinated, the next stage in making seeds is fertilzation. A pollen grain on the flower's stigma sends a tiny tube down the style into the flower's ovary. Inside the ovary are **ovules**, which are tiny plant parts that can become seeds. The pollen tube pierces an ovule and fertilizes it. Now the ovule can grow into a seed.

Fruits for Protection

Once the ovules inside a flower's ovary have been fertilized, they start to grow into seeds.

As the seeds grow, the flower's ovary swells and changes to become a protective case, or covering, called a fruit. As the fruit forms, the flower shrivels and dies.

When we use the word "fruit," we think of a sweet food, such as an apple. A fruit, however, is any kind of outer layer that protects seeds as they grow. Some seeds are protected by soft fruits, such as tomatoes or oranges. Other seeds, such as poppy seeds, grow in hard fruits called capsules or seedpods.

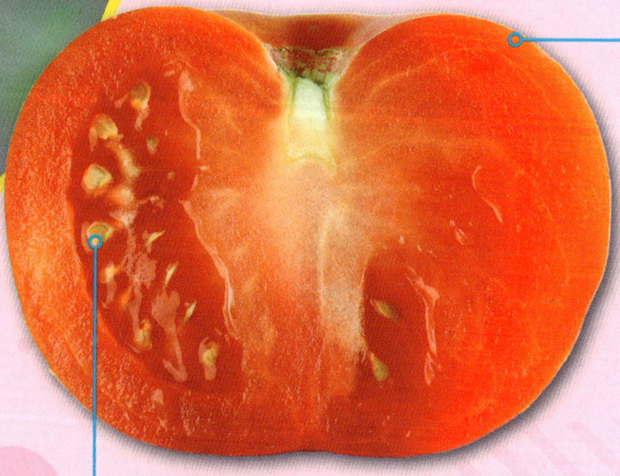

fully formed poppy seedpods

A Close-Up Look at Seeds

The flowers of some plants make thousands of tiny seeds. Other flowers produce just a few large seeds. The seeds of different plants may not look alike, but they all have the same parts.

The outside of a seed is covered by a protective outer layer called the seed coat. Inside a seed is a tiny new plant called an **embryo**. Packed around the embryo is a food supply called the endosperm. This food supply helps the new plant grow.

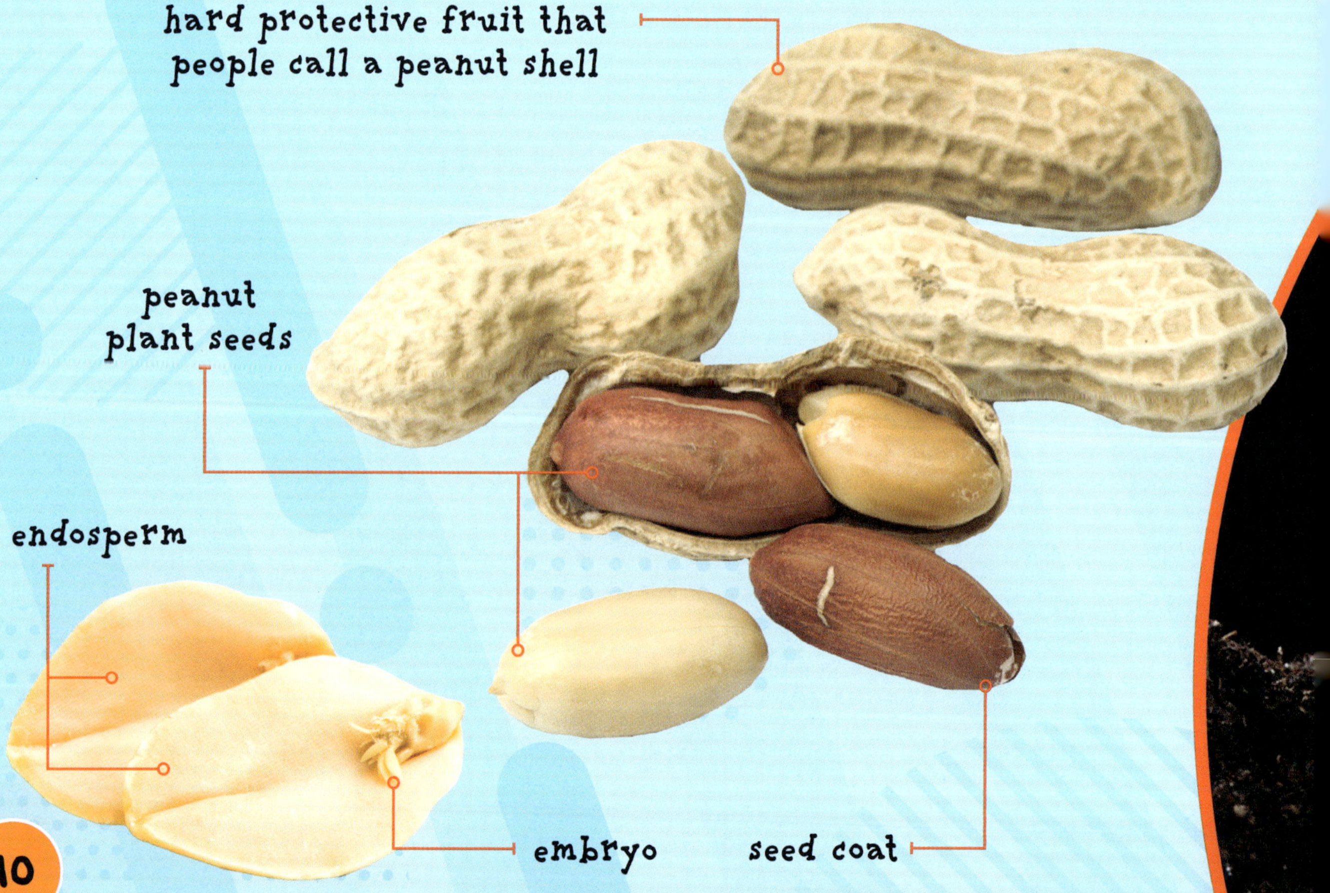

The endosperm of some seeds, such as bean plant seeds, look like tiny leaves. They are called cotyledons or seed leaves. When a new plant emerges from the soil, it's these seed leaves that appear first. The seed leaves continue to feed the tiny, new plant until it grows actual leaves and begins to make its own food.

new bean plant

A Little Seed Leaves Home

To grow successfully, a young plant needs soil to grow in, sunlight, and water and nutrients from the soil. In order to be sure that tiny new plants have enough of all these things, a plant's seeds must move away from the parent plant.

If a new plant, called a seedling, tries to grow in the ground close to its parent plant, however, there may be too much competition between the seedling, the bigger plant, and even other seedlings.

As the young plant grows larger, there may not be enough water and nutrients in the soil to go around. The parent plant may block out sunlight. Therefore, it's important for many types of seeds that they move to new growing places away from their parent plants. How does this happen?

Many seedpods and capsules split open to release their seeds.

a Jimson weed seed capsule

Soft fruits fall from their parent tree and then rot on the ground to release their seeds.

Moving in Droppings and Dung!

Once they fall from a tree or other plant, the protective outer fruits of many seeds quickly become food for animals. Often, animals pick the berries or other fruits directly from a plant. Then the seeds move to a new growing place inside the animals!

Birds, bears, monkeys, and even elephants feed on fruit and also eat the seeds inside the fruit. The animal's body digests the soft fruit, but hard seeds can pass through an animal's **digestive system** unharmed. The seeds then leave the animal's body in its waste and land in a new growing place—often far from the parent plant.

a robin eating berries

black bear droppings containing seeds and undigested berries

Elephants feed on the fruit and seeds of the marula tree. It can take more than 24 hours for the seeds to leave the large animal's body in its dung. In this time, an elephant may have walked miles from the parent marula tree.

Animal Gardeners

Often, seeds such as acorns are moved from place to place by hungry animals in the fall. The animals don't realize they are helping the seeds move to new growing places, but they are!

Chipmunks collect seeds and store them underground in their burrows. During the winter months, which chipmunks spend underground, they feed on this stored food. Not every seed gets eaten, though, and some of the leftover chipmunk food may grow into new plants.

a chipmunk at the entrance to its burrow

A chipmunk can store thousands of seeds each fall.

Squirrels store acorns for winter by burying them. Some of these seeds grow into new oak trees.

Some plants produce seeds with a rich food treat called an elaiosome. Many species of ants collect these seeds and feed the elaiosome to their **larvae**. The rest of the seed is then discarded in the ants' underground nest and may grow into a new plant.

Hitching a Ride

Some seeds travel to new growing places inside animals. Others are buried by them. Some seeds simply hitch a ride to their new home!

The flowers of the burdock plant produce balls of seeds called burrs. Each seed in a burr is armed with a tiny hook. When an animal brushes past the burr, the seeds' hooks attach to the animal's fur or feathers. The seed ball is then pulled from its stem and takes a ride away from its parent plant.

Nicknamed puncture vines, the caltrop plant family produces woody fruits with spikes, or barbs, that look like medieval weapons. The spikes of these fruits can push through skin, clothes, and shoes, and have been known to puncture bicycle tires!

a water caltrop fruit

a cow covered with burrs

Floating on the Wind

Some seeds form inside their flowers and then, when the moment is right, they leave their parent plant by floating on the wind.

Many seeds that are **dispersed** by the wind are tiny and light. Larger and heavier wind-dispersed seeds have wings or other adaptations to help them stay up in the air for as long as possible. This is important because the longer a seed is floating on the wind, the farther from its parent plant it can travel. Maple tree seeds have wings like helicopter blades that help the seeds spin through the air.

A dandelion flower can produce up to 400 seeds. Each seed has a fluffy parachute that catches the wind and helps the seed float to a new growing place.

These tiny foxglove seeds are often dispersed by wind.

Traveling by Rivers and the Sea

It's not only the wind that can carry seeds to a new growing places. Water can do this, too!

Pond irises grow near ponds, lakes, and rivers. When the seedpods of iris flowers split open, the seeds fall into the water. The seeds can then be carried long distances until they become embedded in some mud and start to grow in a new place.

The seeds of some types of palm trees grow inside fruits called coconuts. When these fruits fall from trees that are growing on beaches, they may be carried out to sea. In time, the coconuts are washed up on a different beach, where they can begin to grow in the sand, many miles from their parent tree.

Growing Seeds in Cones

Some types of trees do not grow their seeds in flowers. These trees, such as pine trees, produce seeds in cones.

Like the male and female parts of a flower, pine trees have male and female cones. Male cones produce pollen, which they release into the air. Female cones produce ovules, which are tucked away between their woody, overlapping scales.

Pollen from male pinecones settles on a female cone's scales and fertilizes the ovules. The ovules then develop into seeds. Once the seeds are fully grown, the scales of the female cone open out fully to allow the seeds to fall to the ground.

female pinecone
that's still forming
open female pinecone

scales
seeds

pine tree seeds
hard seed coat

Packed with Power!

Whether a seed is a dust-like speck, a tiny helicopter floating on the wind, or even a spiky hitchhiker riding on a cow, it is packed with the power to produce a new plant.

Most seeds ripen in summer and then separate from their parent plant. Once the seeds are settled in some soil, they wait for spring before starting to grow.

Some plants grow in just a few weeks, produce flowers and seeds, and then die. Others, like giant sequoia trees, may continue to grow for centuries. It's amazing to think that the largest living tree on Earth, the General Sherman giant sequoia, has been growing for more than 2,000 years—and it all began with a tiny seed not much bigger than a grain of rice!

giant sequoia cone

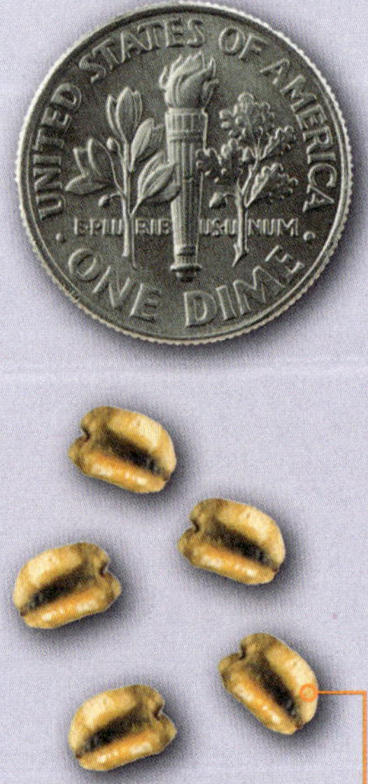

giant sequoia seeds

the General Sherman giant sequoia tree

Let's Investigate Seeds

How do cones protect seeds?

The seeds that are forming inside a female cone must be protected from rain. How does the cone do this? Let's investigate!

YOU WILL NEED:

- a pinecone with open scales
- a jar with a screw-top lid
- water

Step 1:
Place the cone inside the jar.

Step 2:
Fill the jar with water so that the cone is completely submerged, and then screw on the lid.

Step 3:
Keep watch on the cone to see what happens.

Why? How? What?

How did the cone protect its seeds? What will happen if you take the cone out of the water and put it in a warm, sunny spot?
(See page 32 for the answer.)

What happens if a seedling has too much competition?

In order to grow, seeds need sunlight, water, and nutrients. They move to new growing places away from their parent plant and other seedlings to reduce the competition for resources. What happens if a seedling has too much competition? Let's investigate!

YOU WILL NEED:

- two small, empty, clean yogurt cartons
- scissors
- a marker
- potting soil
- bean seeds
- two saucers
- a measuring cup

Step 1:
Use the scissors to pierce three holes in the bottom of each yogurt carton (to allow water to drain through). Label the cartons A and B. *(Only use scissors if an adult is there to help you.)*

Step 2:
Fill each carton three-quarters full with potting soil.

Step 3:
Place five bean seeds on top of the soil in carton A and two bean seeds in carton B. Cover the seeds with more soil, put each carton on a saucer, and then place the cartons in a sunny spot.

Step 4:
Give each carton half a cup of water every other day. The potting soil will contain the nutrients the seedlings need.

Step 5:
When the bean seedlings emerge, remove the weakest-looking seedling from carton B to leave the strongest seedling growing with no competition. Watch how the seedlings grow.

Why? How? What?

Which carton do you think will contain the healthiest plant?
What is happening to the seedlings in carton A?
(See page 32 for the answer.)

Glossary

anther (AN-thur)
A part of a flower that produces pollen.

cones (KOHNZ)
Organs on some nonflowering plants that produce either the pollen or ovules needed for making seeds.

digestive system (dy-JES-tiv SIS-tem)
The group of body parts, including the stomach and intestines, that break down food so that a body can use it for fuel.

dispersed (dih-SPERST)
Spread over a wide area.

embryo (EM-bree-oh)
In plant science, the part of a seed that develops into a plant.

larvae (LAHR-vee)
The young of many types of insects. A larva hatches from an egg.

nutrients (NOO-tree-ents)
Substances needed by a plant or animal to help it live and grow. Plants take in nutrients from the soil using their roots. The nutrients in soil are dissolved in water.

ovary (OH-vuh-ree) The part of a flower where its seeds form.

ovules (AHV-yuhlz) Tiny parts of a plant that become seeds when fertilized by pollen.

pistil (PIS-tuhl) The female reproductive part of a flower. The pistil is made up of the ovary, the style, and the stigma.

pollen (PAH-lin)
A colored dust made on the anthers of flowers, which plants need in order to reproduce.

pollination (pah-lih-NAY-shun)
When pollen is moved from the anthers of one flower to the stigma of another.

seeds (SEEDZ) Parts of a plant that contain all the material needed to grow a new plant.

species (SPEE-sheez) One type of living thing. The members of a species look alike and can reproduce together.

stamens (STAY-munz) The male parts of a flower. Each stamen is made up of a filament and an anther.

stigma (STIG-muh) The part of a flower where pollen must land in order for pollination to happen so that a flower can begin to make seeds.

Websites

www.kew.org/read-and-watch/plant-seed-dispersal-animal-poo

web.extension.illinois.edu/gpe/index.cfm

kids.britannica.com/kids/article/seed/399591

Read More

Huddleston, Emma. *Seed Dispersers: Poop, Fur, and Other Ways Animals Scatter Seeds (Team Earth)*. North Mankato, MN: ABDO Publishing, 2020.

Owen, Ruth. *From Root to Stem: Science and Craft Projects with Seeds and Plants (Crafting with Nature)*. New York, NY: Enslow Publishing, 2023.

Owen, Ruth. *Let's Investigate How Trees Grow (Get Started with STEM)*. Minneapolis, MN: Ruby Tuesday Books, 2022.

Index

Answers

Page 28
As the cone gets wet, its scales will close up tight. This protects the seeds inside from rain. Once the cone gets dry again, the scales will open back up.

Page 29
It's likely that the seedling in carton B will grow faster and look healthier than the seedlings in carton A. The seedlings in carton A are weaker because they are competing for water and nutrients.